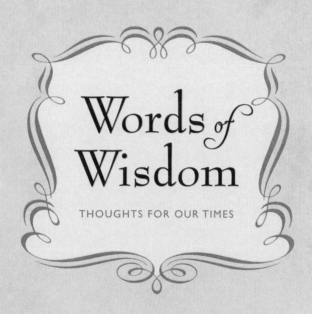

Words *of* Wisdom

THOUGHTS FOR OUR TIMES

ALiCat

Ali☺cat

Alicat Publishing
16 Sandilands Street
South Melbourne VIC 3205
Australia
Email: publishing@alicat.com.au
www.alicat.com.au

Publisher: Ali Horgan
Project Manager: Angie McKenzie
Design: Canary Graphic Design

First published 2011
Printed in China 5 4 3
AC12 337

Contents

Wisdom on Life

Wisdom on Family

Wisdom on Home

Wisdom on Friends

Wisdom on Happiness

Wisdom on Love

Wisdom on Ageing

Wisdom on Marriage

Wisdom on Learning

By three methods we may learn wisdom:
first, by reflection, which is the noblest;
second, by imitation, which is easiest;
and third, by experience,
which is the most bitter.

CONFUCIUS (551 BC–479 BC)
Chinese teacher, philosopher and political theorist

Words of Wisdom

Wisdom has been described as the deep understanding and realisation of people, things, events or situations. Wisdom produces the ability to choose or act consistently and produce optimum results with a minimum of time and energy. Simply, it's making the best of your knowledge.

This deep understanding is what has inspired some people to greatness and to make great judgments. For that reason, wisdom is considered a virtue and the epitome of internal personal success.

It is thought that wisdom comes with experience alone, while free thinkers believe that you can obtain wisdom from a mixture of reason and experience.

The ancient Greeks thought wisdom was a virtue in relation to courage and moderation. Wisdom is the comprehension of what is true and right and the ability to act suitably with that knowledge guiding you.

It is said that you can't put a young head on old shoulders but sometimes, out of the mouths of babes and children, comes wisdom that any adult would be proud of producing. Perhaps it is through their very innocence that wisdom results in their quest for understanding.

As adults, it could be argued that we have lost the ability to think simply and honestly and are floundering in a myriad of complicated calculations and reasoning.

Wisdom is in all of us – we just need to simplify our thought processes and go back to the basics that helped our forefathers survive and grow in an ever changing world. The quotes in this book will show you the way – take heed of their meaning and the insight they provide and pass this on to your children and their children.

You can never overdose on wisdom, you can only be enriched by it.

Knowledge comes, but wisdom lingers.

~◇~

ALFRED LORD TENNYSON (1809–1892)
English poet

Wisdom on Life

What would life be if we had
no courage to attempt anything?

VINCENT VAN GOGH (1853–1890)
Dutch painter

This is the true joy of life,
the being used up for a purpose
recognised by yourself as a
mighty one.

GEORGE BERNARD SHAW (1856–1950)
Irish playwright

Where there is love there is life.

INDIRA GANDHI (1917–1984)
Indian Prime Minister

When I hear somebody sigh,
"Life is hard,"
I am always tempted to ask,
"Compared to what?"

SYDNEY J. HARRIS (1917–1986)
American journalist

It's only when we truly know and understand

that we have a limited time on Earth —

and that we have no way of knowing

when our time is up —

that we will begin to live each day

to the fullest,

as if it was the only one we had.

ELISABETH KUBLER-ROSS (1926–2004)
Swiss-born psychiatrist

Life is meaningless only if we allow it to be.

Each of us has the power to give life meaning,

to make our time and our bodies and our words

into instruments of love and hope.

TOM HEAD (1978–)
American writer

Live every act fully, as if it were your last.

GAUTAMA BUDDHA (563 BC–483 BC)
Spiritual teacher who founded Buddhism

Without some goal and some effort to reach it,

no one can live.

FYODOR DOSTOYEVSKY (1821–1881)
Russian writer and essayist

To be awake is to be alive.

HENRY DAVID THOREAU (1817–1862)
American writer

There is no short cut to achievement.
Life requires thorough preparation –
veneer isn't worth anything.

GEORGE WASHINGTON CARVER (1864–1943)
American scientist and educator

We spend most of our lives
conjugating three verbs:
to want, to have and to do.

EVELYN UNDERHILL (1875–1941)
English writer

There has been much tragedy in my life;

at least half of it actually happened.

MARK TWAIN (1835–1910)
American writer and humorist

Occasionally in life there are those moments of
unutterable fulfilment which cannot be completely
explained by those symbols called words.
Their meanings can only be articulated by the
inaudible language of the heart.

MARTIN LUTHER KING, JNR. (1929–1968)
African-American civil rights leader

The capacity for hope is the most
significant fact of life.
It provides human beings with a sense
of destination
and the energy to get started.

NORMAN COUSINS (1915–1990)
American political journalist and writer

I don't want to get to the end of my life and
find that I lived just the length of it.
I want to have lived the width of it as well.

DIANE ACKERMAN (1948–)
American writer, poet and naturalist

As we express our gratitude,

we must never forget

that the highest appreciation is

not to utter words,

but to live by them.

JOHN F. KENNEDY (1917–1963)
Former President of the United States of America

Listen, are you breathing just a little
and calling it a life?

~⚬⚭⚬~

MARY OLIVER (1935–)
American poet

Intellectual growth should
commence at birth
and cease only at death.

ALBERT EINSTEIN (1879–1955)
German-born American physicist

There are two ways to live: you can live
as if nothing is a miracle; you can live as if
everything is a miracle.

Celebrate the happiness
that friends are always giving,
make every day a holiday
and celebrate just living.

AMANDA BRADLEY
American writer and poet

I have found that if you love life,

life will love you back.

ARTHUR RUBINSTEIN (1887–1982)
Polish-born American composer

If a man is called to be a street-sweeper,

he should sweep streets even as Michelangelo painted,

or Beethoven composed music, or Shakespeare wrote poetry.

He should sweep streets so well that all the host of heaven

and earth will pause to say,

here lived a great street-sweeper who did his job well.

MARTIN LUTHER KING, JNR. (1929–1968)
African-American civil rights leader

Promise yourself to live your life

as a revolution

and not just a process of evolution.

ANTHONY J. D'ANGELO
American writer and educator

I like living. I have sometimes been
wildly, despairingly,
acutely miserable, racked with
sorrow, but through it all
I still know quite certainly that just
to be alive is a grand thing.

AGATHA CHRISTIE (1890–1976)
British writer

To be what we are,

and to become what we are capable

of becoming,

is the only end of life.

ROBERT LOUIS STEVENSON (1850–1894)
Scottish writer and poet

Everything you now do is something you
have chosen to do.
Some people don't want to believe that.
But if you're over age twenty-one,
your life is what
you're making of it.
To change your life, you need to
change your priorities.

JOHN C. MAXWELL (1947–)
American writer, speaker and pastor

Life is something to do when you
can't get to sleep.

FRAN LEIBOWITZ (1950–)
American writer

Life is relationships;
the rest is just details.

GARY SMALLEY (1940–)
American writer and family counsellor

Life's challenges are not supposed
to paralyse you,
they're supposed to help you discover
who you are.

❦

BERNICE JOHNSON REAGON (1942–)
American singer-songwriter and social activist

You learn about equality in history and civics,

but you find out life is not really like that.

ARTHUR ASHE (1943–1993)
American professional tennis player

Each person must live their life as

a model for others.

───✦───

ROSA PARKS (1913–2005)
African-American civil rights activist

Life can only be understood backwards;

but it must be lived forwards.

SOREN KIERKEGAARD (1813–1855)
Danish philosopher, theologian and writer

There are two great rules of life:

never tell everything at once.

❦

KEN VENTURI (1931–)
American professional golfer and broadcaster

Life is a process. We are a process.
The universe is a process.

ANNE WILSON SCHAEF
American writer

Wisdom on Family

In every conceivable manner,
the family is link to our past,
bridge to our future.

ALEX HALEY (1921–1992)
African-American writer

Families are like fudge...
mostly sweet with a few nuts.

AUTHOR UNKNOWN

Families are the compass that guides us.
They are the inspiration to reach great heights
and our comfort when we occasionally falter.

BRAD HENRY (1963–)
American politician

Family: A social unit where the father is concerned with parking space, the children with outer space and the mother with closet space.

EVAN ESAR (1899–1995)
American humorist

Family faces are magic mirrors looking at

people who belong to us,

we see the past, present and future.

GAIL LUMET BUCKLEY (1937–)
American writer

Family is just accident...

They don't mean to get on your nerves.

They don't even mean to be your family,

they just are.

MARSHA NORMAN (1947–)
American playwright and writer

In family life, love is the oil

that eases friction,

the cement that binds closer together

and the music that brings harmony.

⟡

EVA BURROWS (1929–)
Australian Salvation Army officer

Happiness is having a large,
loving, caring,
close-knit family in another city.

GEORGE BURNS (1896–1996)
American comedian, actor and writer

I know why families were created
with all their imperfections.
They humanise you.
They are made to make you forget
yourself occasionally,
so that the beautiful balance of life
is not destroyed.

ANAIS NIN (1903–1977)
French writer

Like all the best families,
we have our share of eccentricities,
of impetuous and wayward youngsters
and of family disagreements.

QUEEN ELIZABETH II (1926–)
British monarch

No matter what you've done for
yourself or for humanity,
if you can't look back on having
given love and attention
to your own family, what have you
really accomplished?

ELBERT HUBBARD (1856–1915)
American writer and philosopher

Other things may change us,
but we start and end
with the family.

— ❦ —

ANTHONY BRANDT
Australian writer

The family – that dear octopus from whose
tentacles we never quite escape, nor,
in our innermost hearts, ever quite wish to.

DODIE SMITH (1896–1990)
English writer and playwright

The only rock I know that stays steady,

the only institution I know that works,

is the family.

———⚮———

LEE IACOCCA (1924–)
American businesswoman

We cannot destroy kindred:
our chains stretch a little sometimes,
but they never break.

MARQUISE DE SÉVIGNÉ (1626–1696)
French aristocrat

What greater thing is there for
human souls than
to feel that they are joined for life –
to be with each other
in silent, unspeakable memories.

GEORGE ELIOT (1819–1880)
English writer

Your family and your love must be
cultivated like a garden.
Time, effort and imagination must be
summoned constantly
to keep any relationship flourishing
and growing.

JIM ROHN (1930–2009)
American entrepreneur, writer and motivational speaker

When you look at your life,
the greatest happinesses are
family happinesses.

JOYCE BROTHERS (1927–)
American psychologist and advice columnist

You don't choose your family.
They are God's gift to you,
as you are to them.

***

DESMOND TUTU (1931–)
South African activist

Home is the place where boys and girls first learn
how to limit their wishes, abide by rules
and consider the rights and needs of others.

SIDONIE GRUENBERG (1881–1974)
American educator

A man travels the world over in search
of what he needs
and returns home to find it.

GEORGE MOORE (1852–1993)
Irish writer and poet

Call it a clan, call it a network,

call it a tribe, call it a family:

whatever you call it, whoever you are,

you need one.

JANE HOWARD (1923–)
English writer

No matter how many communes
anybody invents,
the family always creeps back.

MARGARET MEAD (1901–1978)
American cultural anthropologist

I think people that have a brother or sister

don't realise how lucky they are.

Sure, they fight a lot, but to know that there's

always somebody there, somebody that's family.

TREY PARKER (1969–)
American animator and screenwriter

A family is a unit composed not only

of children but of

men, women, an occasional animal

and the common cold.

❦

OGDEN NASH (1902–1971)
American poet

Rejoice with your family in the
beautiful land of life!

ALBERT EINSTEIN (1879–1955)
German-born American physicist

It is not flesh and blood but
the heart which makes us
fathers and sons.

JOHANN SCHILLER (1759–1805)
German poet and philosopher

The thing about family disasters is
that you never have to wait
long before the next one puts the
previous one into perspective.

⁓⟡⁓

ROBERT BRAULT
American writer

In some families, please is described as
the magic word.
In our house, however, it was sorry.

—∞—

MARGARET LAURENCE (1926–1987)
Canadian writer

If you don't believe in ghosts, you've never been to a family reunion.

ASHLEIGH BRILLIANT (1933–)
English-born American writer and cartoonist

Sometimes our hearts get tangled
and our souls a little off-kilter.
Friends and family can set us right
and help guide us back to the light.

SERA CHRISTANN

In time of test, family is best.

BURMESE PROVERB

The informality of family life is

a blessed condition

that allows us to become our best

while looking our worst.

MARGE KENNEDY (1896–1967)
English writer and playwright

If minutes were kept of a family gathering,
they would show that "Members not Present" and
"Subjects Discussed" were one and the same.

ROBERT BRAULT
American writer

Wisdom on Home

It takes hands to build a house,
but only hearts can build a home.

AUTHOR UNKNOWN

A house is made of walls and beams;

a home is built with love and dreams.

WILLIAM ARTHUR WARD (1921–1994)
American writer

Home is not where you live,
but where they understand you.

CHRISTIAN MORGANSTERN (1871–1914)
German writer and poet

Home is a place you grow up wanting
to leave and grow old wanting to get back to.

～◦◎◦～

JOHN ED PEARCE (1917–2006)
American writer

He is the happiest, be he king or peasant, who finds peace in his home.

JOHANN WOLFGANG VON GOETHE (1749–1832)
German playwright, poet and writer

I long, as does every human being, to be
at home wherever I find myself.

MAYA ANGELOU (1928–)
American poet

Home is where you can say anything you please, because nobody pays any attention to you anyway.

JOE MOORE (1951–)
American educator

There's nothing half so pleasant as
coming home again.

MARGARET ELIZABETH SANGSTER (1938–1912)
American poet and writer

When you're safe at home you wish
you were having an adventure;
when you're having an adventure
you wish you were safe at home.

THORNTON WILDER (1897–1975)
American writer

Home is where you hang your head.

GROUCHO MARX (1890–1977)
American comedian and actor

No matter under what circumstances you leave it,

home does not cease to be home.

No matter how you lived there — well or poorly.

Home is an invention on which no one

has yet improved.

ANN DOUGLAS
American writer

The best way to keep children at home

is to make the

home atmosphere pleasant

and let the air out of the tyres.

❦

DOROTHY PARKER (1893–1967)
American short story writer

A man's home may seem to be his castle
on the outside; inside, it is more often
his nursery.

CLARE BOOTHE LUCE (1903–1987)
American diplomat and playwright

To feel at home, stay at home.

CLIFTON FADIMAN (1904–1999)
American radio host and writer

You can never go home again,
but the truth is you can never leave home,
so it's all right.

MAYA ANGELOU (1928–)
American poet

Where we love is home,
home that our feet may leave,
but not our hearts.

OLIVER WENDELL HOLMES (1841–1935)
American physician

The light is what guides you home,

the warmth is what keeps you there.

～◦～

ELLIE RODRIGUEZ
Cuban-born American journalist

Where thou art – that – is home.

EMILY DICKINSON (1830–1886)
American poet

Home is a shelter from storms –

all sorts of storms.

WILLIAM J. BENNETT (1943–)
American politician and theorist

Love begins at home and it is not

how much we do...

but how much love we put in that action.

MOTHER TERESA (1910–1997)
Armenian-born Catholic nun

The most important work you and I will ever do
will be within the walls of our own homes.

HAROLD B. LEE (1899–1973)
President of the Church of the Latter-Day Saints

My home is not a place, it is people.

LOIS MCMASTER BUJOLD (1949–)
American writer

A man's homeland is wherever
he prospers.

ARISTOPHANES (450 BC–388 BC)
Greek playwright

A house is not a home unless it
contains food and fire
for the mind as well as the body.

❧

BENJAMIN FRANKLIN (1706–1790)
Founding Father of the United States of America

*I believe that being successful means having a balance
of success stories across the many areas of your life.
You can't truly be considered successful in your business life
if your home life is in shambles.*

—◦◦—

ZIG ZIGLAR (1926–)
American writer and motivational speaker

The strength of a nation derives from
the integrity of the home.

~~~

CONFUCIUS (551 BC–479 BC)
Chinese teacher, philosopher and political theorist

Nothing can bring a real sense of security

into the home except true love.

BILLY GRAHAM (1918–)
American Christian evangelist

Any woman who understands the problems
of running a home will be nearer to understanding
the problems of running a country.

MARGARET THATCHER (1925–)
Former Prime Minister of the United Kingdom

You see much more of your children
once they leave home.

LUCILLE BALL (1911–1989)
American comedian and actress

Home is the place where,

when you have to go there,

they have to take you in.

❧

ROBERT FROST (1874–1963)
American poet

A home without books is a body
without soul.

MARCUS TULLIUS CICERO (106 BC–43 BC)
Roman philosopher

Better do a good deed near at home
than go far away to burn incense.

AMELIA EARHART (1897–1939)
American aviation pioneer

I still close my eyes and go home —
I can always draw from that.

DOLLY PARTON (1946–)
American singer-songwriter

Home sweet home.
This is the place to find happiness.
If one doesn't find it here,
one doesn't find it anywhere.

M. K. SONI
American businessman and writer

Most children threaten at times

to run away from home.

This is the only thing that keeps

some parents going.

PHYLLIS DILLER (1917–)
American actress and comedian

Wisdom on Friends

A real friend is one who walks in
when the rest of the world walks out.

WALTER WINCHELL (1897–1972)
American newspaper and radio commentator

True friendship is like sound health;
the value of it is seldom known
until it be lost.

❧

CHARLES CALEB COLTON (1780–1832)
English cleric and writer

Each friend represents a world in us,
a world possibly not born until they arrive
and it is only by this meeting that a new
world is born.

ANAIS NIN (1903–1977)
French writer

My friends are my estate.

EMILY DICKINSON (1830–1886)
American poet

A friend is someone who is there for you

when he'd rather be anywhere else.

‿⧜‿

LEN WEIN (1948–)
American comic book writer

I get by with a little help
from my friends.

JOHN LENNON (1940–1980)
English musician and singer-songwriter

The better part of one's life consists
of his friendships.

ABRAHAM LINCOLN (1809–1865)
Former President of the United States of America

I can trust my friends.
These people force me to examine,
encourage me to grow.

CHER (1946–)
American singer and actor

No love, nor friendship,
can cross the path of our destiny
without leaving some mark on it forever.

FRANCOIS MOCURIAC (1885–1970)
French writer

Friendship is one mind in two bodies.

MENCIUS (372 BC–289 BC)
Chinese philosopher

A friend is someone who knows
the song in your heart
and can sing it back to you when you
have forgotten the words.

AUTHOR UNKNOWN

A friend is a gift you give yourself.

ROBERT LOUIS STEVENSON (1850–1894)
Scottish writer and poet

Friendship with oneself is all-important

because without it

one cannot be friends with anyone

else in the world.

ELEANOR ROOSEVELT (1884–1962)
Former First Lady of the United States of America

The best mirror is an old friend.

GEORGE HERBERT (1592–1633)
Welsh poet

The friendship that can cease

has never been real.

SAINT JEROME (420 BC–347 BC)
Illyrian Catholic priest and apologist

What is a friend? I will tell you...
it is someone with whom you dare
to be yourself.

FRANK CRANE (1861–1928)
Presbyterian minister and columnist

I find friendship to be like wine,
raw when new, ripened with age,
the true old man's milk and
restorative cordial.

THOMAS JEFFERSON (1743–1826)
Former President of the United States of America

My best friend is the one who

brings out the best in me.

HENRY FORD (1863–1947)
American industrialist

*The best way to keep your friends is
not to give them away.*

WILSON MIZNER (1876–1933)
American playwright

*Friendship is always a sweet
responsibility, never an opportunity.*

~⟳~

KAHIL GIBRAN (1883–1931)
Lebanese-American poet and writer

Friends are born, not made.

HENRY ADAMS (1838–1918)
American journalist and writer

One loyal friend is worth ten
thousand relatives.

EURIPIDES (480 BC–406 BC)
Greek playwright

If you make friends with yourself,
you will never be alone.

MAXWELL MALTZ (1927–2003)
American writer

One measure of friendship consists
not in the number of things
friends can discuss, but in the
number of things
they need no longer mention.

CLIFTON FADIMAN (1904–1999)
American radio host and writer

The making of friends, who are real friends,
is the best token we have of
a man's success in life.

EDWARD EVERETT HALE (1822–1909)
American writer and clergyman

The friend who can be silent with us
in a moment of despair or confusion,
who can stay with us in an hour
of grief and bereavement,
who can tolerate not knowing...
not healing, not curing...
that is a friend who cares.

HENRI NOUWEN (1932–1996)
Dutch writer

Sometimes being a friend means
mastering the art of timing.
There is a time for silence.
A time to let go and allow people to hurl
themselves into their own destiny.
And a time to prepare to pick up
the pieces when it's all over.

GLORIA NAYLOR (1950–)
African-American writer and educator

137

Few delights can equal the mere presence of someone we utterly trust.

GEORGE MACDONALD (1824–1905)
Scottish writer and poet

A blessed thing it is for any man
or woman to have a friend,
one human soul whom we can trust utterly,
who knows the best and worst of us
and who loves us in spite of all our faults.

CHARLES KINGSLEY (1819–1875)
British Anglican clergyman and writer

A true friend never gets in your way

unless you happen to be going down.

ARNOLD H. GLASGOW (1905–1998)
American humorist

Don't walk in front of me, I may not follow.

Don't walk behind me, I may not lead.

Just walk beside me and be my friend.

ALBERT CAMUS (1913–1960)
French-Algerian writer and philosopher

Do not protect yourself by a fence,
but rather by your friends.

CZECH PROVERB

When the character of a man is not
clear to you, look at his friends.

JAPANESE PROVERB

Adversity does teach who your
real friends are.

～⚬≫⚬～

LOIS MCMASTER BUJOLD (1949–)
American writer

*We need old friends to help us grow old
and new friends to help us stay young.*

LETTY COTTIN POGREBIN (1939–)
American writer

Depth of friendship does not depend

on length of acquaintance.

RABINDRANATH TAGORE (1861–1941)
Bengali poet and writer

Wisdom on Happiness

Happiness comes when your work and words
are of benefit to yourself and others.

GAUTAMA BUDDHA (563 BC–483 BC)
Spiritual teacher who founded Buddhism

Being happy is something you have to learn.
I often surprise myself by saying "Wow, this is it.
I guess I'm happy. I got a home I love. A career that I love.
I'm even feeling more and more at peace with myself."
If there's something else to happiness, let me know.
I'm ambitious for that, too.

HARRISON FORD (1942–)
American film actor and producer

Since you get more joy out of
giving joy to others,
you should put a good deal of thought
into the happiness
that you are able to give.

ELEANOR ROOSEVELT (1884–1962)
Former First Lady of the United States of America

Joy can be real only if people look upon their life

as a service and have a definite object in life

outside themselves and their personal happiness.

LEO TOLSTOY (1828–1910)
Russian writer

The greatest degree of inner tranquillity

comes from the development of love and compassion.

The more we care for the happiness of others,

the greater is our own sense of well-being.

───⊰◈⊱───

TENZIN GYATSO (1935–)
14th Dalai Lama

Each morning when I open my eyes

I say to myself: I, not events,

have the power to make me happy or unhappy today.

I can choose which it shall be.

Yesterday is dead, tomorrow hasn't arrived yet.

I have just one day, today, and I'm going to be happy in it.

GROUCHO MARX (1890–1977)
American comedian and actor

Hope is itself a species of happiness and, perhaps,
the chief happiness which this world affords.

SAMUEL JOHNSON (1709–1784)
British writer

Knowledge of what is possible is the
beginning of happiness.

GEORGE SANTAYANA (1863–1952)
Spanish-American philosopher and poet

Optimist:
Person who travels on nothing from
nowhere to happiness.

MARK TWAIN (1835–1910)
American writer and humorist

If you want to be happy, set a goal that
commands your thoughts,
liberates your energy and inspires your hopes.

ANDREW CARNEGIE (1835–1919)
Scottish-American businessman and philanthropist

Thousands of candles can be lighted from a single candle and the life of the candle will not be shortened. Happiness never decreases by being shared.

GAUTAMA BUDDHA (563 BC–483 BC)
Spiritual teacher who founded Buddhism

Most people are about as happy as they
make up their minds to be.

ABRAHAM LINCOLN (1809–1654)
Former President of the United States of America

The amount of happiness that you have depends on the amount of freedom you have in your heart.

———— ❧ ————

THICH NHAT HANH (1926–)
Buddhist monk, writer and poet

Happiness is a perfume you cannot pour on others

without getting a few drops on yourself.

⌘

RALPH WALDO EMERSON (1803–1882)

American essayist and poet

My life has no purpose, no direction,

no aim, no meaning,

and yet I'm happy. I can't figure it out.

What am I doing right?

CHARLES SCHULZ (1922–2000)
American cartoonist

Satisfaction of one's curiosity
is one of the greatest sources
of happiness in life.

LINUS PAULING (1901–1994)
American peace activist and writer

To be without some of the things
you want is an indispensable
part of happiness.

BERTRAND RUSSELL (1872–1970)
British philosopher

People say that money is not the key to happiness,
but I always figured if you have enough money,
you can have a key made.

JOAN RIVERS (1933–)
American comedian

Action may not always bring happiness,
but there is no happiness without action.

BENJAMIN DISRAELI (1804–1881)
Former Prime Minister of the United Kingdom
and writer

What everyone wants from life is continuous and genuine happiness.

BARUCH SPINOZA (1632–1677)
Dutch philosopher

Gratefulness is the key to a happy life
that we hold in our hands,
because if we are not grateful,
then no matter how much we have we
will not be happy –
because we will always want to have
something else or something more.

DAVID STEINDL-RAST (1926–)
Austrian-American Roman Catholic theologian

But what is happiness except

the simple harmony

between a man and the life he leads?

ALBERT CAMUS (1913–1960)
French-Algerian writer and philosopher

Happiness cannot be travelled to, owned,

earned, worn or consumed.

Happiness is the spiritual experience of living

every minute with love, grace and gratitude.

DENIS WAITLEY (1933–)
American motivational speaker and writer

The truest greatness lies in being kind,
the truest wisdom in a happy mind.

ELLA WHEELER WILCOX (1850–1919)
American writer and poet

The pursuit of happiness is a most ridiculous phrase,
if you pursue happiness you'll never find it.

C. P. SNOW (1905–1980)
English physicist and writer

If only we'd stop trying to be happy

we'd have a pretty good time.

⁓⟡⁓

EDITH WHARTON (1862–1937)
American writer

Happiness cannot come from without.
It must come from within.
It is not what we see and touch or that which others
do for us which makes us happy;
it is that which we think and feel and do,
first for the other fellow and then for ourselves.

HELEN KELLER (1880–1968)
American writer and political activist

Let us be grateful to people who make us happy;
they are the charming gardeners who
make our souls blossom.

MARCEL PROUST (1871–1922)
French writer and essayist

Happiness is as a butterfly which, when pursued,

is always beyond our grasp,

but which if you will sit down quietly,

may alight upon you.

NATHANIEL HAWTHORNE (1804–1864)
American writer

If you want others to be happy,

practise compassion.

If you want to be happy, practise compassion.

TENZIN GYATSO (1935–)
14th Dalai Lama

Happiness, it seems to me,
consists of two things:
first, in being where you belong,
and second – and best –
in comfortably going through
everyday life, that is,
having had a good night's sleep and
not being hurt by new shoes.

THEODOR FONTANE (1819–1898)
German writer and poet

What we call the secret of happiness
is no more a secret
than our willingness to choose life.

LEO BUSCAGLIA (1924–1998)
American writer and motivational speaker

There is no duty we so underrate as
the duty of being happy.
By being happy we sow anonymous
benefits upon the world.

ROBERT LOUIS STEVENSON (1850–1894)
Scottish writer and poet

We all live with the objective of being happy;
our lives are all different and yet the same.

ANNE FRANK (1929–1945)
German writer and victim of the Holocaust

The true way to render ourselves happy is to love our work and find in it our pleasure.

⸎

FRANCOISE DE MOTTEVILLE (1621–1689)
French writer

People spend a lifetime searching for happiness;
looking for peace. They chase idle dreams,
addictions, religions, even other people,
hoping to fill the emptiness that plagues them.
The irony is the only place they ever needed
to search was within.

RAMONA L. ANDERSON (1887–1949)
American writer

Wisdom on Love

Love is an act of endless forgiveness,
a tender look which becomes a habit.

PETER USTINOV (1921–2004)
English actor and writer

If someone thinks that
love and peace is a cliché
that must have been left behind
in the sixties, that's his problem.
Love and peace are eternal.

JOHN LENNON (1940–1980)
English singer-songwriter

One word frees us of all
the weight and pain of life:
that word is love.

❧

SOPHOCLES (497 BC–406 BC)
Ancient Greek tragedian

Experience is how life catches up
with us and teaches us
to love and forgive each other.

JUDY COLLINS (1939–)
American singer-songwriter

A baby is born with a need to be loved –

and never outgrows it.

FRANK A. CLARK (1911–1991)
American cartoonist

Power without love is reckless and abusive,
and love without power is sentimental and anaemic.

MARTIN LUTHER KING, JR. (1929–1968)
African-American civil rights leader

A life lived in love will never be dull.

LEO BUSCAGLIA (1924–1998)
American writer and motivational speaker

Love many things, for therein lies the true strength,
and whosoever loves much performs much,
and can accomplish much,
and what is done in love is done well.

VINCENT VAN GOGH (1853–1890)
Dutch painter

The only true gift is a portion
of yourself.

RALPH WALDO EMERSON (1803–1882)
American essayist and poet

*Your task is not to seek love, but
merely to seek and find
all the barriers within yourself that
you have built against it.*

MUHAMMAD RUMI (1207–1273)
Persian poet, theologian and mystic

*Love's greatest gift is
its ability to make everything it
touches sacred.*

BARBARA DE ANGELIS (1951–)
American relationship consultant

Why love if losing hurts so much?
We love to know that we are not alone.

C. S. LEWIS (1898–1963)
Irish-born British writer

We look forward to the time when the
power of love will replace the love of power.
Then will our world know the blessings of peace.

WILLIAM E. GLADSTONE (1809–1898)
Former Prime Minister of the United Kingdom

Love and kindness are never wasted.

They always make a difference.

They bless the one who receives them

and they bless you, the giver.

BARBARA DE ANGELIS (1951–)
American relationship consultant

Love is that condition in which the

happiness of another person

is essential to your own.

~⊙⟨⊙~

ROBERT HEINLEIN (1907–1988)
American writer

Wake at dawn with a winged heart
and give thanks
for another day of loving.

KAHIL GIBRAN (1883–1931)
Lebanese-American poet and writer

Love isn't something you find.
Love is something that finds you.

LORETTA YOUNG (1913–2000)
American actress

Love involves a peculiar, unfathomable combination of understanding and misunderstanding.

DIANE ARBUS (1923–1971)
American photographer

Love is the great miracle cure.
Loving ourselves works miracles in our lives.

LOUISE HAY (1926–)
American writer

*Do what you love
and you will find the way
to get it out to the world.*

JUDY COLLINS (1939–)
American singer-songwriter

I love you not only for what you are,

but for what I am when I am with you.

I love you not only for what you have made of yourself,

but for what you are making of me.

I love you for the part of me that you bring out.

ELIZABETH BARRETT BROWNING (1806–1861)
English poet

Love is the child of illusion and
the parent of disillusion.

MIGUEL DE UNAMUNO (1864–1936)
Spanish essayist, writer and poet

If it is your time, love will track you
down like a cruise missile.

⁓⊙⊱⊰⊙⁓

LYNDA BARRY (1956–)
American cartoonist and writer

At the centre of non-violence
stands the principle of love.

MARTIN LUTHER KING, JR. (1929–1968)
African-American civil rights leader

Neither a lofty degree of intelligence
nor imagination
nor both together go to the making of genius.
Love, love, love, that is the soul of genius.

WOLFGANG AMADEUS MOZART (1756–1791)
Austrian music composer

Nobody has ever measured,

not even poets,

how much a heart can hold.

———◦◦◦———

ZELDA FITZGERALD (1900–1948)
American writer

Forgiveness is choosing to love.
It is the first skill of self-giving love.

MOHANDAS K. GANDHI (1869–1948)
Indian civil rights activist and political leader

Flatter me, and I may not believe you.

Criticize me, and I may not like you.

Ignore me, and I may not forgive you.

Encourage me, and I will not forget you.

Love me and I may be forced to love you.

WILLIAM ARTHUR WARD (1921–1994)
American writer

Love is an emotion experienced by the
many and enjoyed by the few.

GEORGE JEAN NATHAN (1882–1958)
American drama critic and editor

Pure love is a willingness to give without a thought of receiving anything in return.

PEACE PILGRIM (1908–1981)
American pilgrim

In the arithmetic of love,

one plus one equals everything,

and two minus one equals nothing.

❧

MIGNON MCLAUGHLIN (1913–1983)
American journalist and writer

There is only one happiness in life,
to love and be loved.

GEORGE SAND (1804–1876)
French writer

Love life and life will love you back.
Love people and they will love you back.

ARTHUR RUBINSTEIN (1887–1982)
Polish-born American composer

The good life is inspired by love
and guided by knowledge.

～◦◦～

BERTRAND RUSSELL (1872–1970)
British philosopher

If you find someone you love in your life,

then hang on to that love.

DIANA, PRINCESS OF WALES (1961–1997)
Member of British Royal Family and humanitarian

The love we give away is the only love we keep.

ELBERT HUBBARD (1856–1915)
American writer and philosopher

Wisdom on Ageing

I'm very pleased to be here.
Let's face it, at my age I'm very pleased
to be anywhere.

GEORGE BURNS (1896–1996)
American comedian, actor and writer

Age is a question of mind over matter.

If you don't mind, it doesn't matter.

⁓⊱∘⊰⁓

MARK TWAIN (1835–1910)
American writer and humorist

Age only matters when one is ageing.
Now that I have arrived at a great age,
I might just as well be 20.

PABLO PICASSO (1991–1973)
Spanish painter and sculptor

I don't believe one grows older.

I think that what happens early on in life

is that at a certain age one stands

still and stagnates.

⸎

T.S. ELIOT (1888–1965)
American poet and playwright

Age is the acceptance of a term of years.

But maturity is the glory of years.

⁓◦⁓

MARTHA GRAHAM (1894–1991)
American dance choreographer

The first sign of maturity is the
discovery that the volume knob
also turns to the left.

—◦◦—

JERRY M. WRIGHT (1941–)
American pastor

The follies which a man regrets
most in his life are those
which he didn't commit when
he had the opportunity.

HELEN ROWLAND (1875–1950)
American journalist and humorist

The great thing about getting older
is that you don't
lose all the other ages you've been.

MADELEINE L'ENGLE (1918–2007)
American writer

The time to begin most things

is ten years ago.

MIGNON MCLAUGHLIN (1913–1983)
American journalist and writer

The older you get, the more you tell it
like it used to be.

⌒⌒⌒

AUTHOR UNKNOWN

The great secret that all old people share is that you really haven't changed in 70 or 80 years. Your body changes, but you don't change at all.

DORIS LESSING (1919–)
British writer

There's always a lot to be thankful for
if you take time to look for it.
For example, I am sitting here
thinking how nice it is
that wrinkles don't hurt.

AUTHOR UNKNOWN

Anyone can get old.

All you have to do is to live long enough.

⌦

GROUCHO MARX (1890–1977)
American comedian and actor

To keep the heart unwrinkled,

to be hopeful, kindly, cheerful, reverent –

that is to triumph over old age.

THOMAS BAILEY ALDRICH (1836–1907)
American poet and writer

He was either a man of about
150 who was rather young for
his years, or a man of about
110 who had been aged
by trouble.

P.G. WODEHOUSE (1881–1975)
English writer

You can live to be a hundred if
you give up all the things
that make you want to live to be a hundred.

WOODY ALLEN (1935–)
American screenwriter, director, comedian and musician

You can only perceive real beauty in
a person as they get older.

ANOUK AIMEE (1932–)
French film actress

You can't hide your true colours as you

approach the autumn of your life.

AUTHOR UNKNOWN

*You know you're getting old when you stoop
to tie your shoelaces and wonder what else you
could do while you're down there.*

GEORGE BURNS (1896–1996)
American comedian, actor and writer

As the arteries grow hard,

the heart grows soft.

H. L. MENCKEN (1880–1956)
American journalist, essayist and satirist

As we grow old…

the beauty steals inward.

RALPH WALDO EMERSON (1803–1882)
American essayist and poet

At twenty we worry about

what others think of us;

at forty we don't care about what

others think of us;

at sixty we discover they haven't been

thinking about us at all.

AUTHOR UNKNOWN

Beautiful young people are
accidents of nature,
but beautiful old people are
works of art.

ELEANOR ROOSEVELT (1884–1962)
Former First Lady of the United States of America

I intend to live forever,
or die trying.

GROUCHO MARX (1890–1977)
American comedian and actor

Age is something that doesn't matter,
unless you are a cheese.

❦

BILLIE BURKE (1884–1970)
American actress

In a dream you are never eighty.

ANNE SEXTON (1928–1974)
American poet

Grandchildren don't make a man feel old;
it's the knowledge that
he's married to a grandmother.

⁓◦⊙◦⁓

AGATHA CHRISTIE (1890–1976)
British writer

Middle age is when you choose cereal
for the fibre, not the toy.

AUTHOR UNKNOWN

Once you're over the hill,

you begin to pick up speed.

❧

CHARLES M. SCHULZ (1922–2000)
American cartoonist

It's a sobering thought that when
Mozart was my age
he had been dead for two years.

TOM LEHRER (1928–)
American singer-songwriter and satirist

We don't stop playing because we grow old,

we grow old because we stop playing.

GEORGE BERNARD SHAW (1856–1950)
Irish playwright

No one is ever old enough
to know better.

HOLBROOK JACKSON (1874–1948)
British journalist and writer

The joy of being older is that in
one's life one can,
towards the end of the run,
overact appallingly.

QUENTIN CRISP (1908–1999)
English writer and raconteur

If I had my life to live over again,
I'd make the same mistakes —
only sooner.

TALLULAH BANKHEAD (1902–1968)
American actress and talk show host

Growing old is mandatory;

growing up is optional.

CHILI DAVIS (1960–)
West-Indian professional baseball player

In a man's middle years there is
scarcely a part of the body
he would hesitate to turn over to
the proper authorities.

~∞∾~

E.B. WHITE (1899–1985)
American writer

To what do you attribute your long life?
To the fact that I haven't died yet.

SIR MALCOLM SARGENT (1895–1967)
English conductor, organist and composer

Everyone is the age of their heart.

GUATEMALAN PROVERB

Wisdom on Marriage

Newlyweds become oldyweds,
and oldyweds are the reasons that families work.

AUTHOR UNKNOWN

I love being married.
It's so great to find that one special
person you want
to annoy for the rest of your life.

RITA RUDNER (1953–)
American comedian, writer and actress

Marriage is an alliance entered into by a man
who can't sleep with the window shut
and a woman who can't sleep with the
window open.

GEORGE BERNARD SHAW (1856–1950)
Irish playwright

Chains do not hold a marriage together.
It is threads, hundreds of tiny threads which
sew people together through the years.

SIMONE SIGNORET (1921–1985)
French actress

Whatever you may look like,

marry a man your own age —

as your beauty fades,

so will his eyesight.

PHYLLIS DILLER (1917–)
American actress and comedian

An archaeologist is the best husband

a woman can have;

the older she gets,

the more interested he is in her.

AGATHA CHRISTIE (1890–1976)
British writer

Never get married in the morning,

because you never know who

you'll meet that night.

⁓⊰⊱⁓

PAUL HORNUNG (1935–)
American professional footballer

One advantage of marriage is that,

when you fall out of love with him

or he falls out of love with you,

it keeps you together until you fall in again.

JUDITH VIORST (1931–)
American writer and journalist

A successful marriage requires
falling in love many times,
always with the same person.

MIGNON MCLAUGHLIN (1913–1983)
American journalist and writer

Marriage is a book of which
the first chapter is
written in poetry and the remaining
chapters in prose.

BEVERLEY NICHOLS (1898–1983)
English writer

Love is a flower which turns into
fruit at marriage.

FINNISH PROVERB

Love seems the swiftest but it is
the slowest of all growths.
No man or woman really knows
what perfect love is
until they have been married
a quarter of a century.

MARK TWAIN (1835–1910)
American writer and humorist

A first-rate marriage is like a first-rate hotel: expensive, but worth it.

MIGNON MCLAUGHLIN (1913–1983)
American journalist and writer

Here's to matrimony, the high sea for which

no compass has yet been invented!

HEINRICH HEINE (1797–1856)
German poet, journalist, essayist and literary critic

Don't marry the person you think you can live with;

marry only the individual you think you can't live without.

JAMES C. DOBSON (1936–)
American evangelical Christian writer and psychologist

Only choose in marriage a man
whom you would choose as a friend
if he were a woman.

JOSEPH JOUBERT (1754–1824)
French essayist

A happy marriage is the union
of two good forgivers.

RUTH BELL GRAHAM (1920–2007)
American writer and poet

A perfect marriage is one in which
"I'm sorry" is said just often enough.

MIGNON MCLAUGHLIN (1913–1983)
American journalist and writer

The highest happiness on earth is marriage.

WILLIAM LYON PHELPS (1865–1943)
American writer, critic and scholar

I have learned that only two things are necessary
to keep one's wife happy.
First, let her think she's having her own way.
And second, let her have it.

LYNDON B. JOHNSON (1908–1973)
Former President of the United States of America

A happy marriage is a long conversation
which always seems too short.

~≈∞≈~

ANDRE MAUROIS (1885–1967)
French writer

A man without a wife is like a vase

without flowers.

～∘⊙∘～

AFRICAN PROVERB

Marriage is popular because it combines the maximum of temptation with the maximum of opportunity.

GEORGE BERNARD SHAW (1856–1950)
Irish playwright

Marriage is the agreement to let a family happen.

BETTY JANE WYLIE (1931–)
Canadian writer and playwright

The world has grown suspicious of anything

that looks like a happily married life.

OSCAR WILDE (1854–1900)
Irish poet, writer, dramatist and critic

To be happy with a man you must
understand him a lot and love him a little.
To be happy with a woman you must
love her a lot and not try to understand her at all.

HELEN ROWLAND (1875–1950)
American journalist and humorist

Wisdom on Learning

A single conversation with a wise man is better
than ten years of study.

CHINESE PROVERB

You can teach a student a lesson for a day;
but if you can teach him to learn
by creating curiosity,
he will continue the learning process
as long as he lives.

CLAY P. BEDFORD
American businessman

Get over the idea that only children
should spend their time in study.
Be a student so long as you still
have something to learn
and this will mean all your life.

HENRY L. DOHERTY (1870–1939)
American businessman

It's what you learn after you know it all
that counts.

HARRY S. TRUMAN (1884–1972)
Former President of the United States of America

In the spider web of facts,

many a truth is strangled.

PAUL ELDRIDGE (1888–1982)
American poet, short story writer and teacher

When the student is ready, the master appears.

BUDDHIST PROVERB

Give me a fruitful error any time,

full of seeds, bursting with its own corrections.

You can keep your sterile truth for yourself.

VILFREDO PARETO (1848–1923)
Italian engineer, sociologist, economist and philosopher

Education consists mainly of
what we have unlearned.

MARK TWAIN (1835–1910)
American writer and humorist

Man's mind, once stretched by a new idea,
never regains its original dimensions.

OLIVER WENDELL HOLMES (1841–1935)
American physician

The most useful piece of learning
for the uses of life is to unlearn
what is untrue.

ANTISTHENES (445 BC–365 BC)
Greek philosopher

Some people will never learn anything…
because they understand everything too soon.

ALEXANDER POPE (1688–1744)
English poet

You learn something every day
if you pay attention.

RAY LEBLOND

I am always ready to learn although
I do not always like being taught.

WINSTON CHURCHILL (1874–1965)
Former Prime Minister of the United Kingdom

Always walk through life as if you have

something new to learn and you will.

VERNON HOWARD (1918–1992)
American spiritual teacher, writer and philosopher

Learn as much as you can while you are young,

since life becomes too busy later.

DANA STEWART SCOTT (1932–)
American mathematician and computer scientist

The man who is too old to learn was
probably always too old to learn.

HENRY S. HASKINS